3496 8726

NATURE CLOSE-UP

TADPOLES

TEXT BY ELAINE PASCOE

PHOTOGRAPHS BY DWIGHT KUHN

BLACKBIRCH PRESS, INC.

WOODBRIDGE, CONNECTICUT

Published by Blackbirch Press, Inc.
260 Amity Road
Woodbridge, CT 06525

Printed in the United States

10 9 8 7 6 5 4

To my brother Byron   To S.M.S.
–D.K.   –E.P.

front cover: tadpole with four legs
back cover: (left to right) wood frog tadpole, wood frog tadpole with four legs, wood frog tadpole climbing out of the water, adult wood frog

Library of Congress Cataloging-in-Publication Data
Pascoe, Elaine.
Tadpoles / by Elaine Pascoe. — 1st ed.
      p.   cm. — (Nature close-up)
   Includes bibliographical references (p. 47) and index.
   Summary: Explores the physcial characteristics, reproduction, habitat, and metamorphosis of tadpoles. Includes hands-on activities.
   ISBN 1-56711-179-3 (alk. paper)
   1. Tadpoles—Juvenile literature. 2. Frogs—Juvenile literature. 3. Tadpoles—Experiments—Juvenile literature. [1. Tadpoles. 2. Tadpoles—Experiments. 3. Experiments. 4. Frogs] I. Title. II. Series: Pascoe, Elaine. Nature close-up.
QL668.E2P34   1997   95-40848
597.8'90439—dc20   CIP
                                                                     AC

Note on metric conversions: The metric conversions given in Chapters 2 and 3 of this book are not always exact equivalents of U.S. measures. Instead, they provide a workable quantity for each experiment in metric units. The abbreviations used are:

cm	centimeter	**kg**	kilogram
m	meter	**l**	liter
g	gram		

Contents

A Tadpole's Double Life

A chorus of croaks and peeps fills the cool night air—a sure sign of spring: In ponds and marshy places, frogs are awake after their long winter rest. They are ready to begin one of the most remarkable life cycles of any creatures on Earth.

Frogs are amphibians—they belong to a special group of animals. The word *amphibian* comes from Greek words meaning "double life," and these animals really do lead two lives. In the first stage of life, frogs are tadpoles and must live entirely in water. Later, as adults, they can breathe and live on land—although most frogs are never far from water.

Biggest and Smallest

North America's largest frog, the bullfrog, grows up to 8 inches (about 20 cm) long. The largest frog in the world is the Goliath frog, which lives in West Africa. It can measure 1 foot (about 30 cm) long and weigh up to 6 pounds (almost 3 kg). The smallest frogs are Cuban tree frogs, which are barely half an inch (about 1 cm) long.

The bullfrog is North America's largest frog.

This American toad belongs to one of about 20 different families of frogs and toads found throughout the world.

Some scientists think that amphibians are a link between water-dwelling animals, such as fish, and land dwellers, which breathe air. Perhaps amphibians developed from fish, and then land-dwelling animals developed from amphibians. Certainly frogs are among the oldest living things. There were frogs on Earth 180 million years ago. And while dinosaurs and many other creatures appeared and disappeared, frogs remained.

Today frogs—and toads, their close relatives—live in nearly every part of the world, except the polar regions. There are hundreds of different kinds, but scientists group them into about 20 families.

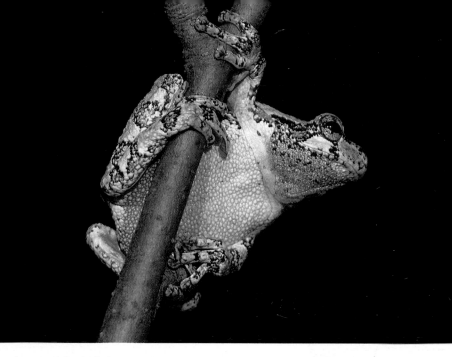

The leopard frog (left) is a true frog; the gray tree frog (above) and the spring peeper (below) are tree frogs.

Frog Families

Most North American frogs belong to the true-frog and tree-frog families. True frogs include the bullfrog, the wood frog, the green frog, the pickerel frog, and the leopard frog. These frogs usually live in or near water. Their hind feet are webbed to help them swim, and their long, powerful hind legs allow them to jump huge distances.

Tree frogs also live near water. But, as you can guess, they spend much of their time in trees. Sticky pads on their toes act like suction cups to help them cling to branches and leaves. They can even cling to glass! North American species include the green, gray, California, and canyon tree frogs and the spring peeper. They are all small frogs. Most grow to be only about 2 inches (5 cm) long.

Left: Tiny suction cups on their toes make tree frogs great climbers.
Below: True frogs have webbed hind feet.

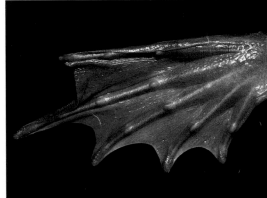

Compared to the toad at right, this wood frog is sleek.   **The skin of the American toad is very bumpy.**

Toads also live throughout North America. How do you tell a frog from a toad? It isn't easy—the terms aren't precise. Even scientists don't always agree on whether one species or another should be considered a frog or a toad, and many consider all these animals to be frogs. But as most people use the terms, toads differ from true frogs and tree frogs in several ways: Toads spend more of their adult lives out of water. They are squatter and heavier-looking than frogs. And, while a frog's skin is moist and smooth, a toad's skin is dry and covered with warty-looking bumps.

An old belief states that touching a toad will give you warts. That's not true—but most toads do secrete a foul, toxic substance. It makes the toad taste terrible to predators such as birds, snakes, and raccoons. Most predators quickly learn to avoid toads.

9

Because they don't have to worry so much about predators, toads are not as shy as frogs. You can often see toads in lawns and gardens, searching for an insect meal. It's harder to see a frog—usually, you just hear a soft "plop" as the frog disappears into its pond when you approach. A startled frog can leap several feet (about a meter), perhaps ten times its body length, in a rush to safety.

Dangerous Colors

While North American frogs are drab, some frogs in other parts of the world are brilliant shades of yellow or red. Their bright colors are a warning—these frogs secrete poisons on their skin. Poisonous frogs include the dart-poison frog of South America, whose skin secretions are so deadly that Indians coat the tips of their hunting arrows with them.

This gray tree frog is very hard to see against its surroundings.

One reason that frogs are hard to spot is that most are well camouflaged, which means they are colored to blend in with their surroundings. Often, frogs that live in ponds or high in trees are green, while those that live in woodland undergrowth or on the ground may be mottled shades of gray, green, or brown. This camouflage coloring makes it hard for predators to find frogs—and it helps the frogs lie hidden from insects and other prey they hope to catch.

11

How Frogs Live

Adult frogs spend most of their time looking for food. Their huge, bulging eyes let them see all around as they constantly scan their surroundings for their next meal. Insects and earthworms make up most of their diet, but a frog will eat just about anything that moves and fits in its mouth.

When a frog spots a likely meal, it flicks its long tongue out like a whip and catches the prey on the tongue's sticky tip. In a flash, the tongue folds back into the mouth, bringing dinner with it. If you watch a frog eat, you'll see it close its eyes when it swallows. This is because it's actually pushing down with its big eyeballs, to help force the food down its gullet. But you won't see a frog drink water. Nearly all frogs absorb water through their skin instead of drinking it—so they must always be in damp surroundings.

Top: **A frog actually uses its eyes to push food down its gullet.**
Bottom: **Bullfrogs often eat earthworms.**

Frogs must also be in warm surroundings. They are cold-blooded—their body temperature goes up and down with the temperature of the air (or water) around them. This means that in cold climates, frogs must find a way to survive through winter. Many hibernate in the mud at the bottom of ponds. When a frog hibernates, its body systems slow down so much that it doesn't need to eat or even to breathe air. It absorbs the little bit of oxygen that it needs from the water, through its skin. When spring comes and the water starts to warm up, the frog wakes and swims to the surface to breathe.

A bullfrog hibernates in the mud.

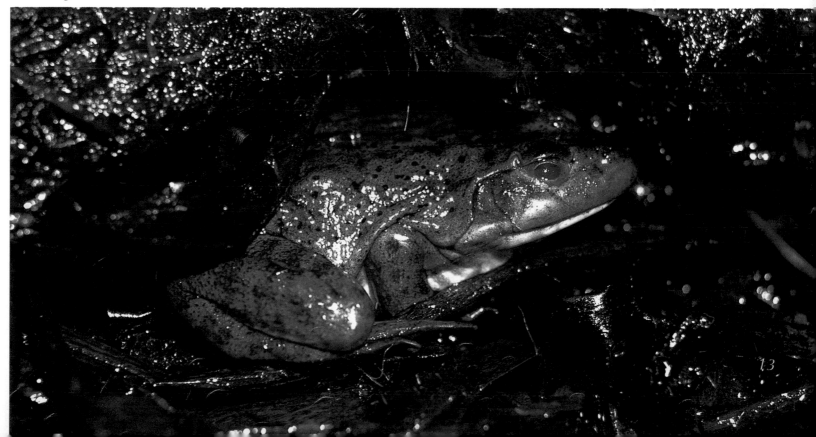

Tadpole to Frog

The chorus of peeping and croaking that announces spring is made by male frogs, which wake up first. Males have a pouch, or vocal sac, in the throat; by filling it with air, they can make loud sounds that can be heard nearly a mile (1.6 km) away. Each kind of frog has its own call. The green frog's is a loud "plunk," while male bullfrogs seem to call "jug-jug-jug-o-rum." When females hear the calls, they go to find a mate of their species.

Usually, the male is calling from a good spot at the edge of a pond. Even if they spend most of their adult life on land, almost all frogs and toads must find a pond or some other body of water in which to reproduce. This is also true of salamanders, the other major group of amphibians.

The female frog lays its eggs, usually in the water, and the male fertilizes them. Most frogs are poor parents—once the eggs are laid, they swim away. The eggs are surrounded by a jellylike substance that protects them. Together, the blob of eggs and jelly is called frog spawn. The female lays lots of eggs, sometimes thousands. But most of the eggs are eaten by fish and other predators.

A male spring peeper calls to a female.

A female frog lays eggs, and then a male fertilizes them.

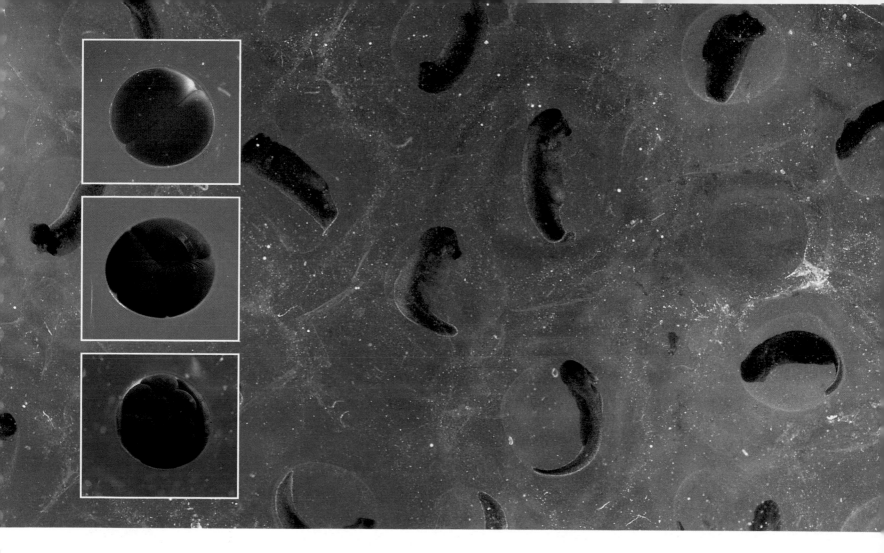

The eggs that survive change from a single cell—or living unit—into two cells (top), then four cells (middle), and so on. Finally, they develop into tiny tadpoles, which hatch and start to swim right away. They look nothing like their parents—they look like fish. A tadpole has no legs; instead, it has a tail for swimming. And instead of lungs for breathing air, it has gills for breathing underwater, like a fish.

Tadpoles spend their first few weeks (or months, depending on the kind of frog) swimming around their pond, eating algae and other plants. All the while they are changing.

First, hind legs begin to grow.

Then, the front legs appear.

The eyes grow bigger, the mouth begins to grow wider, and the tail starts to shorten.

There's a lot going on inside, too. Lungs develop, and the gills disappear. Now, the tadpole must come to the surface to breathe. Its digestive system begins to change, too.

Finally, the froglet is nearly ready to hop out of the pond on four legs. It begins to leave the water for short periods of time. In the last stage of the change, or metamorphosis, it stops eating for a while. Instead of using energy from food, it uses the energy stored in its long tadpole tail, which shrinks away. The froglet is now a frog.

Frog Fathers

A few types of frogs help protect their eggs and tadpoles. The oddest of these is the Darwin's frog of South America. Females of this species lay eggs on land, and several males gather around the eggs. Each male swallows some of the eggs, letting them slip into his vocal sac. Inside the sac, the eggs hatch into tadpoles and develop into froglets. Then, one day, the froglets jump out of their father's mouth!

Frogs and People

Frogs and toads are a great help to people. They eat many insects that might otherwise damage crops. And researchers have found that the chemicals frogs secrete on their skin can often be used in medicine. Chemicals produced by frogs have been used to fight skin and eye infections, for example.

People haven't been so helpful to frogs, however. The number of frogs worldwide has been declining sharply since the 1980s. Salamanders also seem to be in trouble. Scientists aren't sure why this is happening, but they think that environmental problems may be behind the disappearance of these animals.

In many areas, the ponds and marshy areas where frogs live have been drained or filled because people want to use the land for farming or construction. Acid rain, produced by pollution from automobiles and factories, may be killing some frogs. When frogs absorb water through their thin skin, they also absorb whatever chemicals and pollutants may be in the water.

Some scientists believe that frogs are also being harmed by ultraviolet radiation from the sun. Earth is protected from most of this harmful radiation by a layer of ozone gas in the atmosphere. The ozone screens out ultraviolet radiation before it can reach Earth. But now pollution has caused the ozone layer to grow thinner, so more ultraviolet radiation is getting through. And research has shown that frogs' eggs don't hatch when they are exposed to too much ultraviolet light.

Toads help people by eating potato beetles and other insects that damage crops.

Researchers are trying to find out what is behind the declining numbers of these animals. They hope that, if they find the answers, they'll be able to help one of Earth's oldest creatures survive.

2

Collecting and Caring for Frog Eggs and Tadpoles

It's fascinating to see tadpoles grow into frogs. Often, you can find frog eggs or tadpoles in the wild and bring them home to watch the process firsthand. (Adult frogs are difficult to care for. It's best not to collect them.) Remember that the number of frogs is declining worldwide, however. To help make sure that as many tadpoles as possible grow up to be frogs, follow these rules:

- Always take just a few eggs or tadpoles.
- Care for them well, following the guidelines given here. If you do, your tadpoles will have as good a chance of growing into frogs as tadpoles in the wild—perhaps better, because they will be safe from predators.
- When you've finished watching them, take them back to the spot where you found them and release them.

You can also purchase frog eggs from sources such as those listed on page 47.

What You Need:

* A mop or broom handle
* Black electrical tape
* A large food strainer, or something else to form a net: a small mesh laundry bag or the leg from an old pair of tights. If you use fabric rather than a food strainer, you'll also need:
* A wire clothes hanger
* Needle and thread

Equipment for Collecting

To gather tadpoles or frog eggs, you'll need a long-handled collecting net and a container in which to carry your finds. You can buy a collecting net, but it's easy to make one.

What to Do:

Tape the food strainer tightly to the mop handle. Or, if you're using fabric, do this:

1. Bend the clothes hanger to form a round loop. Straighten the hanger's hook. (Ask an adult to help if the hanger is hard to bend.)
2. Put your bag or fabric through the loop, so that it forms a pouch about 12 inches (30 cm) deep. If you are using a section of material cut from an old pair of tights, sew the bottom of the pouch closed.
3. At the open end, fold the fabric over the wire loop, and sew it in place.
4. Tape the net to the handle.

Your container can be any sort of wide-mouthed plastic pail or jar, deep enough (or with a lid) to keep water from slopping out when you carry it. Fill the container with pond water at the collecting site. You may also find it helpful to bring along a shallow, light-colored container, such as a dishpan or an old food keeper. If you empty your net into the flat pan first, it will be easy to see and sort out debris and water creatures that you don't want. Then you can put only the material that you do want in your collecting jar.

When and Where to Search

Spring is the best time to find eggs and tadpoles because that's when frogs generally lay their eggs. The eggs hatch quickly, and the tadpoles of most species grow into frogs in just a few weeks. Later in the year, you may still find the tadpoles of bullfrogs, which take two to four years to reach adulthood, and green frogs, which will not become adults until the following year. These large tadpoles (with bodies the size of a grape or bigger) are best left in the wild—they need a pond-sized habitat in which to grow up.

Look for eggs and tadpoles in shallow, quiet, fresh water—along the edges of ponds and marshes, in shallow garden pools, even in ditches and other temporary wet spots that dry up in summer. When you visit a pond or a marsh, take an adult with you, and follow these steps for safety:

- Wear old sneakers or sandals for wading—don't go barefoot because glass or sharp stones may be hidden under the water.
- Use your net handle or another pole to test the depth of the water ahead of you, to be sure that the bottom doesn't drop off suddenly.
- Avoid streams with fast-running currents—they can be dangerous, and you won't find eggs or tadpoles there.
- Don't hunt for eggs and tadpoles from a boat or wharf—you might fall in deep water.

Frog eggs look like little black balls or seeds, encased in jelly. You'll generally find them in masses that may contain dozens, hundreds, even thousands of eggs. Don't take all the eggs—scoop up a dozen or so with your net, and put them in your collecting container.

Hunt for tadpoles where water plants grow. Tiny tadpoles are hard to spot. But if you sweep your net through a clump of water plants, you may catch some even without seeing them. Collect just a few tadpoles, and put some pond plants in your container along with them.

This spotted salamander larva might eat your frog tadpoles if it is placed in the same container.

Compare this wood frog tadpole to the similar-looking salamander larva on the left.

To make sure that your tadpoles and frog eggs arrive home safely, follow these steps:

- Make sure that other pond animals don't end up in the container with the tadpoles or the eggs; small fish and other water creatures may eat them. Some large tadpoles will eat small tadpoles, too—so gather tadpoles that are all about the same size.
- Use a large collection container with plenty of pond water.
- Don't let the container sit in direct sunlight, which can heat the water and harm your tadpoles.
- Cover the container only to carry it. Otherwise, leave the cover off, so that air can reach the water surface.

Caring for Eggs and Tadpoles

You'll need to set up a more permanent container to keep eggs or tadpoles for a period of time. If you collect both eggs and tadpoles, put them in separate containers. Use a small aquarium, a large glass jar, or a plastic food-storage container. Leave the container uncovered.

Fill the container with pond water or spring water. Most tap water contains chlorine, which will harm tadpoles. The water will be safe to use only if you treat it with chlorine remover (available in pet stores) or let it stand for 24 hours before adding it to the container, so that the chlorine disappears. The water should be at room temperature. Keep the container out of direct sunlight and away from heat sources, such as radiators.

Add some pond plants to your tadpole container (and to your egg container when the eggs begin to hatch, which in most cases will be within a week or two). Don't crowd the tadpoles—you'll be able to keep five or six in a 1-gallon (4-l) container. If you've collected eggs, keep just a few of the tadpoles that hatch. Return the rest to the pond where you found the eggs.

An aquarium works well as a container for eggs or tadpoles.

It's hard to tell one kind of tadpole from another, so you may not know just what you've got until the little creatures begin to grow into frogs. As a rule, true-frog and tree-frog tadpoles are brown or gray and take one to three months (or more, for certain types) to grow into frogs. Toad tadpoles are often black and grow out of the tadpole stage more quickly.

In the wild, tadpoles eat algae and other plant matter. To feed them at home, tear some lettuce or spinach leaves into pieces about 1 inch (2–3 cm) across, and ask an adult to boil the pieces for one minute. You can also add a pinch of cornmeal to the tadpole container. Once the tadpoles grow legs, they start to develop a taste for protein. Add a small piece of liver or a bit of hard-cooked egg yolk, along with cornmeal and other foods. Every day, be sure to remove any food that the tadpoles didn't eat, so that it won't rot.

Tadpoles make a lot of waste. Change the water every day (always using chlorine-free water). Or remove waste from the bottom of the container by sucking it up with a clean meat baster. Use a small food strainer or an aquarium net to transfer tadpoles from one container to another.

When the tadpoles grow four legs, they will need to climb out of the water—they are getting ready to breathe air and search for food above the surface. Lily pads, a floating piece of plastic or wood, or a partly submerged branch or rock will give them a way to get out of the water when they want to. Gradually, they'll spend more and more time above the surface.

When they have four legs, their tails are nearly gone, and they're spending most of their time out of water, the new frogs are ready for life on land. It's best to release them now. Take them back to the pond where you found them as eggs or tadpoles or, if that's not possible, to another place with suitable water.

Keeping Frogs

Once they are ready for life on land, frogs are difficult to keep. They are shy creatures that need a lot of moisture, and they must have living, moving food. Even toads, which aren't as shy and can survive in drier conditions than true frogs and tree frogs, prefer meals that move. If you can't release your frogs right away, you can keep them for a short time in a vivarium—a container that you set up for them. But you will have to supply them with a diet of live insects.

Use a large container, such as a 10-gallon (38-l) aquarium, for a vivarium. Put a smaller plastic container filled with chlorine-free water on one side. The water should be deep enough for the frogs to submerge themselves. Put a layer of soil several inches (8–12 cm) deep on the other side. Add moss and plants for shelter and shade.

Keep the soil moist. The plants need moisture—and so do the frogs. Mist the contents of the vivarium daily with a household plant mister, or partly cover the vivarium with a sheet of Plexiglas to keep moisture inside. Don't completely cover the container, though, because the frogs need fresh air. Ask an adult to help you make a screen top, to keep the frogs (and their food) from jumping or climbing out.

Large frogs will eat live mealworms, small earthworms, flies, crickets, and other moving insects. Toads are fond of slugs. Small frogs must be fed small insects, such as fruit flies. Collect fruit flies by luring them with rotting fruit, or buy them from biology supply houses such as those listed on page 47.

You can catch a variety of insects with a net. Follow the instructions for a tadpole-collecting net, but in place of mesh use a closely woven fabric such as muslin (see photo right). Sweep the net through grass or over a garden to collect small insects and spiders. Add them to the vivarium to feed your frogs.

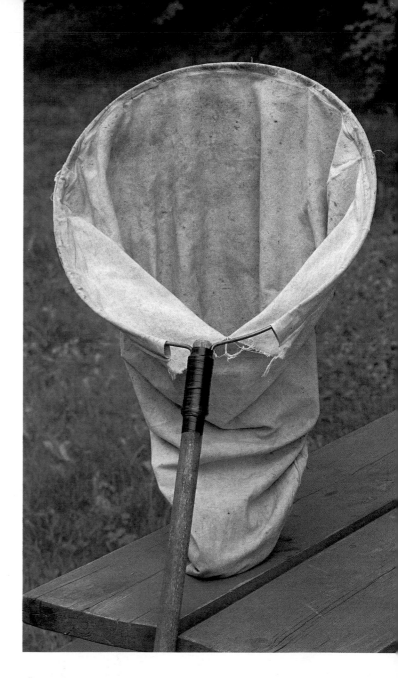

Handle the frogs as little as possible. Always wet your hands before picking up a frog, and cup your hands around it gently. And always wash your hands after touching a toad or a frog. Toads and some North American frogs secrete substances that can irritate your eyes, if you should touch your eyes before washing your hands. (Some frogs from other parts of the world secrete deadly poisons, but you're not likely to see those frogs—except maybe in a zoo or an exotic pet store. If you do travel to foreign countries, use extreme caution with any frogs you encounter.)

As soon as you can, return your frogs to the wild. They'll be happier there. And by releasing them, you'll help make sure that there will be a new crop of tadpoles next spring.

Always release your frogs into a suitable habitat.

3

Investigating Tadpoles

Tadpoles thrive when they have the food and surroundings that they like best. In this chapter, you'll find activities that will help you learn more about these tiny animals and the conditions they need. Have fun with these activities, but remember that you are working with living creatures. Disturb the tadpoles as little as possible when you set up your experiments and projects and when you move them from one container to another. Remember to keep their containers out of direct sunlight. Change the water or remove wastes daily, and feed the tadpoles appropriate food, as described in Chapter 2.

What You Need:

* Several tadpoles, all the same size
* Two identical plastic containers or jars
* Clear container, for measuring tadpoles
* Pond water or chlorine-free tap water (see Chapter 2)
* Spinach, lettuce leaves, or cornmeal (see Chapter 2)
* Graph paper

What Temperatures Are Best for Tadpoles?

In many areas, the water in ponds and marshes is quite cold in early spring. It warms up later in the year. Do tadpoles grow better in cold water, or are they more likely to thrive at warmer temperatures? Decide what you think, based on what you've read about tadpoles. Then do this experiment to find out if you are right.

What to Do:

1. Fill both containers with water to the same level, and add an equal number of tadpoles to each.
2. Place one container indoors, where it will be at room temperature (but not in sunlight). Place the second container in a cold place, such as a cool basement or a refrigerator.
3. Other than temperature, try to keep conditions the same for the tadpoles in both containers. Put an equal amount of cornmeal or boiled spinach or lettuce in each container, and remove any uneaten food when you change the water.
4. Watch the tadpoles to see how they grow. Once a week, estimate the tadpoles' length. You can do this easily by putting a clear container filled with chlorine-free water on a sheet of graph paper. One by one, put the tadpoles in the clear container and note how many squares each tadpole covers. Then return them to their original containers. Keep a record of your findings.

Results: Did the tadpoles in one container grow more quickly than in the other? Did legs appear sooner in one container?

Conclusion: Was your prediction correct? What do your results tell you about the conditions that tadpoles need in the wild?

You can do the same experiment with frog eggs, to see if they hatch more quickly in cold water or warmer water. Be sure to use eggs that you found in a clump—that way, you'll know that they were all laid at the same time. You don't need to add food until the eggs hatch.

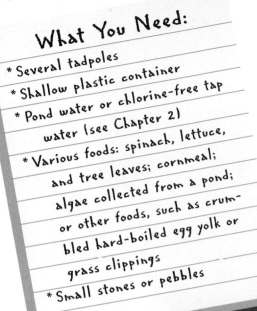

What You Need:

* Several tadpoles
* Shallow plastic container
* Pond water or chlorine-free tap water (see Chapter 2)
* Various foods: spinach, lettuce, and tree leaves; cornmeal; algae collected from a pond; or other foods, such as crumbled hard-boiled egg yolk or grass clippings
* Small stones or pebbles

What Do Tadpoles Like to Eat?

Tadpoles spend most of their time searching for and eating food. Do you think that they prefer one sort of food over another? Do this activity to find out.

What to Do:

1. Fill the container with pond water or chlorine-free tap water, and add the tadpoles.
2. Tear spinach, lettuce, or tree leaves into pieces about 1 inch (2–3 cm) across, and ask an adult to help you boil the pieces for one minute. Let the pieces cool.
3. Add equal amounts of the leaves and other foods to the tadpole container, placing each in a different spot. Put pebbles on the leaf pieces to hold them in place. Sprinkle cornmeal and egg yolk on the water surface.
4. Watch the tadpoles for several days to see what they eat. Remember to change the water and replace the uneaten foods daily.

Results: Did the tadpoles prefer one food over another? Repeat this activity in a few weeks, when the tadpoles have grown legs. Do they prefer the same foods?

Conclusion: Based on your results, what foods to you think tadpoles search out in the wild?

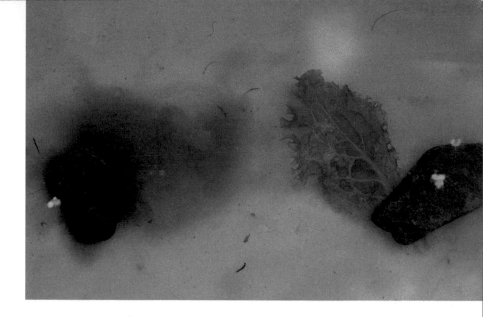

What You Need:

* Several tadpoles
* Tall, clear container
* Pond water or chlorine-free tap water (see Chapter 2)
* Pieces of boiled spinach or lettuce (see Chapter 2)
* Wire clothes hanger or thin stick, longer than the container is deep
* Four clothespins
* Six straight pins, pushpins, or thumbtacks

Where Do Tadpoles Like to Feed?

Some water creatures always feed near the surface. Others, such as catfish, hunt for food at the bottom of ponds. And some can be found feeding at middle depths. Where do you think tadpoles prefer to feed? Here's a way to find out.

What to Do:

1. Fill the container with the water and add several tadpoles.
2. Put the stick or clothes hanger in the jar, so that one end of it rests on the bottom. (You may need to flatten the clothes hanger, or ask an adult to help you cut it.) Clip it to the rim of the container with a clothespin.
3. Using the straight pins, pushpins, or thumbtacks, attach a piece of spinach (or lettuce) to each of the three remaining clothespins.
4. Clip the clothespins to the stick so that one is near the surface, one is at the bottom, and one is in the middle.
5. Check the container a few times a day for several days, to see where the tadpoles feed.

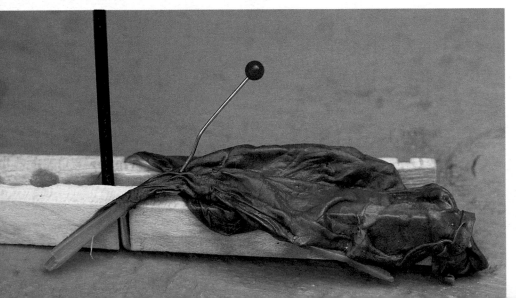

Results: At which level did you see the tadpoles feeding most often?

Conclusion: Based on your results, what part of a pond to you think tadpoles are most likely to prefer—surface water, deeper water, or the bottom?

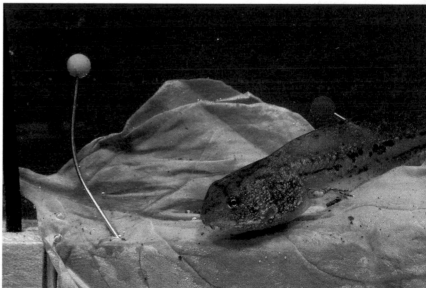

What You Need:

* Clear plastic container
* Pond water or chlorine-free tap water (see Chapter 2)
* Several tadpoles
* Bright flashlight

Are Tadpoles Attracted to Light?

On warm summer nights, you can often find toads near porch lights and other outdoor lights. Do you think that tadpoles are also drawn to light? Try this activity to see. If you can, do it in a dimly lit room.

What to Do:

1. Fill the container with water and add the tadpoles. (If you are already keeping tadpoles in a clear container, you do not need to move them to another container for this activity.)
2. Place the flashlight next to the container, with the light shining on one side of it. (Use a flashlight rather than an electric lamp for this activity. If a lamp were to accidentally come in contact with water, it could deliver a deadly electrical shock.)
3. Watch the tadpoles.

Results: Do the tadpoles swim toward the light or move away from it?

Conclusion: What do your results tell you about tadpoles and light? Can you think of ways in which the tadpoles' reaction to light helps them in the wild? Why do you think adult toads are drawn to lights at night?

Do Tadpoles Like to Hide Under Cover?

Will tadpoles seek shelter under lily pads and other kinds of cover, or will they prefer to swim in open water? Make a prediction, and then do this activity to see if you are right.

What to Do:

1. Fill the container with water and put in the tadpoles.

2. Place food in the container, making sure that you put the same amount and kind of food on both sides of the container. Use pebbles to hold lettuce and similar foods in place.

3. Put the cover over one side of the container, or float lily pads or tree leaves on the water surface at one side.

4. Watch the tadpoles over several days, to see where they spend their time.

Results: Each time you check the container, note where you find the tadpoles. Keep a record of your results.

Conclusion: Was your prediction correct? Why do you think the tadpoles acted as they did?

What You Need:
* Shallow plastic container
* Pond water or chlorine-free tap water (see Chapter 2)
* Several tadpoles
* Lily pads, tree leaves, or a dark-colored cover large enough to fit over half the container (a piece of cardboard will do)
* Food for the tadpoles (such as boiled lettuce or spinach or other items listed in Chapter 2)

More Tadpole Activities

1. Keep a tadpole notebook. Include dates, notes, and drawings. Every few days, observe the tadpoles and record the changes that are taking place. Measure the tadpoles as described on pages 34–35 ("What Temperatures Are Best for Tadpoles?"). Note new features, such as legs, as they begin to appear, and make drawings of the tadpoles as they change. Record changes in their behavior, too—for example, when they begin to breathe air at the surface.

To measure a tadpole, place it in a clear jar, and then put the jar on a piece of graph paper.

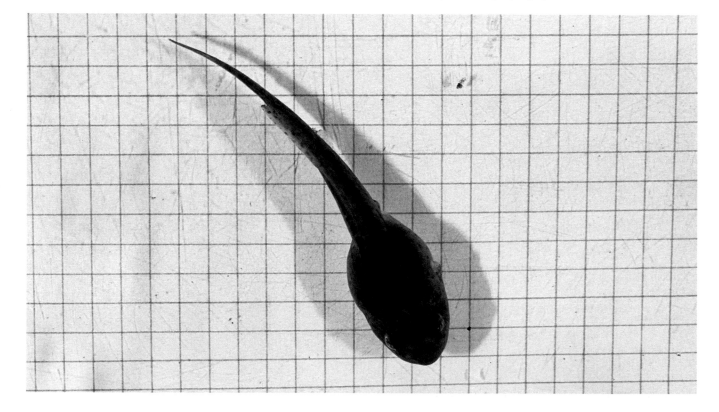

2. See if you can figure out what kind of eggs or tadpoles you've collected. As a rule, toads lay their eggs in long strings, and frogs lay their eggs in big blobs. Toad tadpoles are usually small and black, and they grow into little toads very quickly. But identifying tadpoles more specifically isn't easy, because different species look so much alike. Check in your library for field guides to amphibians, some of which have keys to tadpole identification. As the tadpoles grow up and develop frog features, it will become easier to identify them.

3. Use a magnifying glass to examine frog eggs close up. Inside the jelly that surrounds each egg is a dark area—the developing tadpole. Check the eggs each day for changes. At first, the dark areas will be round. When the eggs are five to ten days old, the tadpoles inside will have developed heads and tails, so that the dark areas look like little commas. Then, the tadpoles begin to wiggle. If conditions are right, they will hatch a week or two after the eggs were laid.

43

Results and Conclusions

Here are some possible results and conclusions for the activities on pages 34 to 41. When you do these activities, you may not get the same results. Many things can affect the way tadpoles grow and behave. If your outcomes differ, think about the reasons. What do you think led to your results? If you can, repeat the activity and see if the outcome is the same.

What Temperatures Are Best for Tadpoles?

You'll probably find that tadpoles do best in water that is kept at room temperature. They grow less quickly in cold water. This is also the case with frog eggs, which are slower to hatch at cold temperatures.

What Do Tadpoles Like to Eat?

Tadpoles eat plants. In the wild, they eat mainly algae, but they will eat other plant material that is soft enough for them to take into their mouths (they don't have teeth). After their legs develop and their digestive systems start to change, they will eat protein foods such as egg yolk or liver. When tadpoles are nearly grown into frogs, they stop eating for a while. Then, as frogs, they become insect eaters.

Where Do Tadpoles Like to Feed?

In aquariums, most tadpoles prefer to feed near the bottom. But they will swim to areas where they find the most plants, and this means that they're often found in shallow water along the edges of ponds.

Are Tadpoles Attracted to Light?

Tadpoles aren't drawn to light. They may swim away from it or try to hide from it because sunlight can be harmful or because predators would see them more easily in strong light. Adult toads go toward lights at night because they find insects there.

Do Tadpoles Like to Hide Under Cover?
Tadpoles usually seek the shelter of pond plants or other cover. This helps them avoid predators, and they find more food in plant-filled areas than in open water.

45

Some Words About Frogs and Tadpoles

algae: Simple plants that grow mostly in water. Some kinds of algae float in the water; others grow on underwater rocks or on other water plants.

amphibians: A group of animals that, with a few exceptions, spend part of their life in water and part of their life on land. All amphibians have backbones and are cold-blooded. Their young live in water and breathe with gills, while adults, which have lungs, generally live on land and breathe air.

camouflage: A coloring or pattern that blends in with the surroundings.

cells: Very small, often microscopic units, that compose living things.

cold-blooded: Having a body temperature that fluctuates with the temperature of the surrounding air or water.

chlorine: A chemical used to purify drinking water.

gills: Body organs that draw oxygen from water.

gullet: Throat.

habitat: The place where a plant or animal naturally lives.

hibernate: To pass the winter in a dormant, or resting, state.

metamorphosis: A process through which immature animals take on a different form to become adults.

spawn: Masses of eggs laid in water.

species: A class of living organisms that have the same characteristics.

vivarium: A tank containing a complete habitat for frogs or other animals, with soil, plants, rocks, water, and so on.

vocal sac: An expandable pouch in a male frog's throat. By filling the pouch with air, the frog can make loud calls that are heard by female frogs far away.

Sources for Frog Eggs and Tadpole Supplies

These companies sell frog eggs and other materials through the mail. If you raise tadpoles obtained through mail-order sources such as these, be sure to release the adult frogs only in suitable ponds or other habitats.

Carolina Biological Supply
2700 York Road
Burlington, NC 27215
1-800-334-5551

Connecticut Valley Biological
82 Valley Road, P.O. Box 326
Southampton, MA 01073
1-800-628-7748

Insect Lore
P.O. Box 1535
Shafter, CA 93263
1-800-LiveBug

For Further Reading

Clarke, Barry. *Amazing Frogs and Toads.* New York: Knopf, 1990.

Gibbons, Gail. *Frogs.* New York: Holiday House, 1993.

Julivert, Marcia A. *The Fascinating World of Frogs and Toads.* Hauppague, NY: Barron's, 1993.

Lacey, Elizabeth A. *The Complete Frog: A Guide for the Very Young Naturalist.* New York: Lothrop, Lee & Shepard, 1989.

Lovett, Sarah. *Extremely Weird Frogs.* Santa Fe, NM: John Muir, 1991.

Pfeffer, Wendy. *Frogs and Tadpoles.* New York: HarperCollins Children's Books, 1994.

Ricciuti, Edward. *Amphibians.* Woodbridge, CT: Blackbirch Press, 1993.

White, William. *All About the Frog.* New York: Sterling, 1992.

Index

Note: Page numbers in italics indicate pictures.